CW01335723

MAU MAU RE▔▔▔

A History from Beginning to End

Copyright © 2020 by Hourly History.

Table of Contents

Introduction

The Mau Mau Rebellion, also known as the Mau Mau Uprising, took place in Kenya between 1952 and 1960. It was a conflict between Kenyan peoples—primarily from the Kikuyu tribe—and Great Britain.

Kenya had been a British colony since 1920 and under formal British control since 1895. The conflict began when members of several tribes joined to form the Kenya Land and Freedom Army (KLFA), a revolutionary force which formed in opposition to colonial rule by Great Britain. Initially, the fighting was sporadic, but as Britain came to recognize the uprising as a threat to their interests, military action was ramped up.

The British responded to the Mau Mau Rebellion, whose tactics were mainly guerilla fighting, in three ways. First, they descended on the city of Nairobi to find and relocate any and all possible Mau Mau fighters and sympathizers (they primarily targeted Kikuyu people). Second, they attempted land reform, as land distribution was a major cause of discontent among Kenyans. Finally, they initiated a resettlement plan, called the villagization program. This program would outlast the others, as Kenyans—primarily Kikuyu—were housed in everything from settlements to concentration camps, depending on their revolutionary leanings.

The Mau Mau Rebellion was a very violent conflict. Several massacres took place, and many civilians were killed. Both sides of the conflict used abhorrent torture techniques. In 2012, Great Britain admitted to committing war crimes during the uprising, though more than likely, both sides were guilty.

The Mau Mau Uprising also divided the Kenyan people, both inter- and intra-tribally. The British very much exploited the differences between tribes to their advantage. The Mau Mau Rebellion exacerbated these conflicts, which in turn created issues in the new country of Kenya once Britain granted independence in 1963.

Unlike other rebellions and revolutions in global history (particularly in the twentieth century when many former European and American colonies fought for independence), historians still disagree on whether the Mau Mau Uprising was an actual revolutionary movement or not. In fact, Kenyans themselves still have a difficult time locating it within their national story.

Regardless of the varying interpretations among historians, the Mau Mau Uprising is certainly a key event not only in Kenyan history but in the history of British colonialism and African history in general. It has a complicated and nuanced story, as well as a conflicted legacy.

Chapter One

Background and Causes

"One hundred sixty Gusii have not been killed outright without any further casualties on our side. . . . It looks like a butchery. . . . Surely it cannot be necessary to go on killing these defenseless people on such an enormous scale."

—Winston Churchill

The British had claimed the region known as Kenya as a protectorate in 1895, solidifying their presence there. It did not become a formal colony, though, until after World War I in 1920.

The British were not a welcome presence in the region by the native inhabitants. From the start, the native peoples in the area, comprised of various localities and tribes, fought against British incursions. There were at least four unsuccessful armed uprisings against British imperial rule in the region of Kenya before the Mau Mau Uprising, the first beginning immediately before 1895. By far, casualties from these uprisings were on the Kenyan side; superior weaponry and lack of concern for Kenyan life led to several massacres. The sheer brutality involved in suppressing these uprisings was in itself a cause of the Mau Mau Rebellion, and one of the reasons it became such a bloody conflict.

The reason the British were so interested in Kenya was its land: Kenya contained very fertile soil, ideal for growing. Thus, the British encouraged their own people to settle and farm the land, essentially establishing plantations. In order for them to do this, though, the British had to clear the land, which meant removing the Kenyan people already living and farming there, effectively stealing their land from them. The British then wanted the displaced Kenyans to become laborers on what was previously their own land, and sometimes Kenyans were coerced or forced into doing so. Obviously, from the beginning, both the land seizure and forced labor created great discord between the colonizers and the colonized.

The seizure of land was the chief complaint on the part of the Kenyans against the colonial administration for most of its tenure. By the 1930s, Britain recognized the danger this posed to maintaining peace in the region and introduced some land reforms. It was, however, too little too late. By that point in time, the land seizure was so complete that the most fertile areas of Kenya—the Rift Valley and Central Provinces—were referred to as the "White Highlands" because they had been so heavily settled by white Europeans. In the land reform initiatives, Britain reapportioned some land to the native Kenyan peoples, but it was a fraction, per capita, of what white settlers received. In addition, it was almost entirely in the less fertile, less lucrative regions. The land reform, in the end, did not pacify the rebellious undertones in Kenya, as Britain would learn in ensuing uprisings, including the Mau Mau Rebellion.

There were other issues during British colonial rule that also contributed to unrest among Kenyans. Primarily, these dealt with how the Kenyan people themselves were treated. Almost immediately upon full colonial rule in 1920, the British government began making all Kenyan men above the age of fifteen carry a form of government identification, called a *kipande*. This document contained basic information about the carrier, including name, date of birth, and fingerprints. However, in practice, this document served to restrict the ability of native-born Kenyans to move from region to region. This meant that their ability to seek better employment, or more available land, or travel for any other reason, was extremely limited.

The kipande played into another issue that Kenyans had with the colonial government: wages. Once displaced from their land, Kenyans were encouraged, and sometimes forced, to become wage laborers. The British government passed several laws and imposed taxes early in the twentieth century that tied Kenyans to their regions and prohibited movement. The kipande was one of these measures. The wages paid to most laborers were barely sufficient to support an individual, let alone a family. What was more, conditions were often very poor. Laborers were forced to work long hours in whatever weather. British settlers and their white staff were also allowed to use physical force and beatings to coerce laborers. The fact that their movement was so restricted virtually eliminated their options to escape poor conditions and seek a living elsewhere.

Despite these early measures, British settlers still had trouble recruiting enough labor. The system of labor and farming became a vicious cycle: labor shortages and high demand caused landowners to use harsher and harsher methods in order to coerce greater output; but with worsening conditions, laborers' lives became less and less tolerable, and they continued to resist conscription into such brutal conditions. The rate of production that the settlers expected from their laborers demanded so much work that it was often more than the available labor was capable of handling. Settlers and landowners turned to the British, who imposed more and more legislation and colonial policies that limited Kenyans' movement and forced them into employment on white farms.

Finally, other policies and practices hurt the Kenyan peoples and contributed to the growing resentment between them and the British. Kenyans were taxed heavily, and the use of their tax dollars was a further issue. In large part, Kenyans wound up paying for services that benefited the while settlers much more than themselves. Their money built roads and railroads and supported other systems that allowed the large-scale farms of the white settlers to function. At the same time, the colonial administration ignored the needs of Kenyans. Medical care, education, and other social services remained substandard or non-existent. Meanwhile, the white settlers were taxed at much lower rates. This led many Kenyans to realize that they were being forced—through their labor and their earnings—to support a foreign class living much better than they were and making enormous profits off of their suffering on top of it.

One tribe that was particularly impacted by the presence of the British was the Kikuyu, and they would be very active in the KLFA and the Mau Mau Uprising. The Kikuyu tribe was a dominant presence in the highlands, some of the land most desired by Europeans. Therefore, they were often victims of British land and labor policies. Despite restrictions on movement, many Kikuyu people fled the plantations and headed for the cities, mainly Nairobi, which would make Nairobi a hotbed of revolutionary unrest. The migration was so widespread, in fact, that the Kikuyu contributed to doubling Nairobi's population in just over ten years, by 1952. This movement into Nairobi would place the city at the center of the early years of the Mau Mau Uprising.

In some ways, migration fractured the Kikuyu. Some members, however, managed to hold onto their land or acquire new land. These wealthier members of the tribe alienated themselves from their fellow tribesmen, preferring to ally themselves with the British colonial authorities. This created both a tangible and intangible distancing among the tribe, which would worsen during the uprising.

The global context in which this rebellion took place is also very important in order to fully understand why both parties acted in the ways that they did. In the decades following World War II, a period of worldwide decolonization took place. During this time, countries and regions that had been under colonial rule (usually by European nations or the United States) achieved independence. Sometimes this independence was given by the colonial power, and sometimes it came through armed struggle. As Kenyans watched many fellow African countries and countries around the world being granted statehood and home rule, they, too, desired the same.

However, at the same time, the Cold War was also occurring and greatly impacted the decolonization process. During the Cold War, capitalist countries, particularly the United States and Great Britain, opposed communist world powers, especially the USSR (Russia) and China. As countries gained independence and established governments, it was imperative to capitalist countries that they remain capitalist, and to communist countries that they align with communism. The Cold War was often fought in proxy conflicts over these sorts of alliances. The capitalist west aggressively fought communist uprisings around the world—sometimes directly and sometimes indirectly—while communist powers often supported communist upstarts and helped them rise up and take governments around the world.

Any uprising or revolutionary movement of any kind was seen through this dichotomous lens of east versus west, communist versus capitalist. It became very difficult for either side in the Cold War struggle to fathom an in-between, or to consider that perhaps the causes were more complex. Thus, when the Mau Mau Rebellion began in Kenya, Great Britain worried that Kenya was being influenced by communism and communists. Keeping control was not only important to the British for economic reasons, but for the containment of communism worldwide. In the end, it would also contribute to the decision to grant independence.

By 1952, the stage was set for a clash between the British and their colonial peoples in Kenya. The conflict would be long and bloody and permanently change the social, cultural, and economic landscape of the region.

Chapter Two

The Desire for Freedom

"Whilst they could not be expected to take kindly at first to a departure from their traditional way of life, such as living in villages, they need and desire to be told just what to do."

—Statement from Kenya's Colonial Ministers, 1954

The use of the name "Mau Mau" is in itself indicative of some of the issues that not only led to the conflict, but that would continue to plague both the Mau Mau movement and the nation of Kenya once it was formed. The region of Kenya was not a traditional country in the western sense of the word. Part of the process of colonization—and decolonization—was the imposition of new borders and boundaries that did not take tribal or local allegiances and affiliations into consideration. What this meant was that the colonizing powers drew new demarcations that separated some tribes or local communities, or lumped different peoples together, who had perhaps fought one another in the past, or did not have the same language, religion, and customs.

The origin of the term "Mau Mau" remains a mystery and reflects this amalgamation of cultures. The term sounds like different words or phrases in different tribal languages and dialects. Neither participants, nor their descendants, nor historians, nor linguists can be quite sure about the exact origins of the term. This reflects the fact that the movement itself was a product of chaos and dislocation caused by colonialism, as well as the coming together of different people against a common enemy. Many of the fighters actually preferred the term Kenyan Land and Freedom Army.

The Mau Mau Uprising was not the first time that a more widespread, inter-tribal alliance was attempted in Kenya or the first time that Kenyans tried to stop Great Britain. Even before 1895, the people of the Kenyan region greatly resisted Britain's movement into their homeland. Almost certainly, Great Britain committed atrocities during their campaigns to subjugate the fertile farmland in Africa.

The Nandi Resistance began in 1890 and lasted sixteen years, making it the longest continuous conflict against British imperialism at the end of the nineteenth century. The Nandi people were led by an Orkoiyot, who was at once a religious, political, and military leader. The Orkoiyot at the helm of the Nandi Resistance was Koitalel Arap Samoei. The insurgency he led was only ended when he met with a British colonel on false pretenses: he believed he was meeting to discuss a truce, but instead, he and everyone accompanying him were slaughtered, effectively ending the Nandi Resistance.

The Giriama Uprising broke out less than a decade later, in 1913. The Giriama tribe was (and is) one of the largest ethnic groups in Kenya, living in the coastal region. This rebellion was led by a woman, Mekatilili Wa Menza, who was celebrated as a great prophet of her people. She began the rebellion after becoming incensed by the demands of the colonial administration (legend holds that she publicly slapped a British official in the face). Devoutly religious, she rallied others (including the mostly male tribal leaders) to her cause, and they vowed to resist British colonialism by whatever means necessary. The British responded by burning Giriama homes and seizing their land. Even though Mekatilili Wa Menza was sent to prison, she escaped twice and traveled back to her people both times. She died among them in 1924.

A couple of decades later, insurgency would make its home among the Kikuyu people, and they would become the key actors in the Mau Mau Rebellion. In 1947, a group of Kikuyu women rose up against the forced labor policies of the British. Additionally, in 1950, a group of the Pokot tribe in the Central Province rallied behind a Kenyan man named Lukas Pkech. In a confrontation with British troops, Pkech and nearly thirty other men armed with spears were shot and killed by British troops. Less an uprising than an incident, this kind of violent retaliation on the part of the British against Kenyan unrest served to further alienate them from Kenyans.

Action toward independence was also tried through politics rather than armed insurgency, particularly in the decade before the Mau Mau Uprising began. In 1944, Harry Thuku, a Kenyan politician, helped form the Kenyan African Study Union (KASU). Born in central Kenya, Thuku had been involved in similar initiatives in the past. Also a member of the Kikuyu tribe, he was a founding member of the Young Kikuyu Association, East African Association, and the Kikuyu Provincial Association, and former president of the Kikuyu Central Association.

The KASU was relatively unsuccessful and short-lived, and Thuku resigned as chairman not long after its founding. Historians are not in agreement about why he did so, but one possible reason is that it became too militant, foreshadowing the coming armed insurgency of the KLFA. Once World War II ended, Kenyan soldiers who had fought for Great Britain in the war returned home expecting pay, at the very least. When their payments were delayed and they were passed over for medals in recognition of service in favor of white soldiers, their anger against Britain only mounted, and many began to see armed rebellion as the only way to affect real change.

Over the course of the next several years, the Mau Mau came together gradually. It was composed primarily of people from the Kikuyu, Embu, and Meru tribes. Just as there was no formal call for troops, there was no formal declaration of independence or war that began the Mau Mau Rebellion, and in fact, some historians mark the beginning with separate incidents. This relative confusion is not helped by the fact that the British governor of Kenya, Phillip Mitchell, retired in 1952, and in the months prior to his retirement largely ignored the growing movement. His replacement would arrive not even aware that an active rebellion was occurring. The Mau Mau Uprising may have begun when the process of oathing, a long-standing African tribal tradition, became radicalized. Alternatively, the beginning may be marked on October 3, 1952, when a group of Mau Mau fighters killed a European woman by stabbing her in Thika, a city northeast of Nairobi.

Regardless of establishing an exact date for the start of the uprising, six days after the stabbing of the woman, there was no doubt that the Mau Mau were in open rebellion against Great Britain. On October 9, 1952, Mau Mau fighters killed Senior Chief Waruhiu. While this man was Kenyan, he was closely allied with the British and supported the colonial administration. In addition, the manner in which he was killed served to reinforce the status of revolt: he was shot in broad daylight, in sight of many witnesses.

After the assassination of Waruhiu, Evelyn Baring, the British governor of Kenya, requested that a state of emergency be declared. He did not arrive in Kenya until shortly before this happened, and he was given no information before he arrived at his post that Kenya was in open rebellion. His request was honored (eventually), and the Mau Mau Uprising was officially recognized as a threat to the British Empire.

Chapter Three

The Early Months of the Uprising

"[The Mau Mau are] an irrational force of evil, dominated by bestial impulses and influenced by world communism."

—John Colin Carothers

One aspect that tends to be a hallmark of colonialism is a sort of paternalistic racism. In the case in Kenya, many British people believed that the Kenyans were of lower intellectual capacities than the British. In their view, the Kenyans were incapable of learning, progressing, or fighting on par with their superior colonizers. This false sense of superiority, however, would prove to be an impediment to the British during the Mau Mau Rebellion. In fact, many of the leaders of the uprising were well-educated. What was more, they were learned in military history and they were charismatic. They also deeply understood the plight of their fellow Kenyans and established customs and rules that helped them maintain very strong loyalty among their ranks.

One popular decision made by the leaders of the uprising early on was the incorporation of women. They recognized that women could be key to certain aspects of the war. Women helped supply the Mau Mau fighters with not only food, medicine, and arms, but they also provided them with information. The British officials and their Kenyan allies did not suspect women (at least not initially), and therefore they were able to acquire information and carry supplies without being detected. In a remarkable move, some women also served in the fighting. What was more, the inclusion of women helped the Mau Mau maintain loyalty: when women became so deeply involved, the uprising became a family affair. Everyone who would be included in the new order once the British were gone had a role to play. Later in the war, however, brutality (particularly sexual assault) against women was a hallmark of the Kenyan Home Guard, a militia unit composed of loyalist Kenyans organized by the British. It placed Mau Mau fighters in staunch opposition to their counterparts.

Mau Mau leadership were realistic about their military potential against the might of the British, particularly General Gatunga (not to be confused with the Gatunga settlement in Kenya). He recognized that from a strictly military standpoint, his forces were out-numbered and out-gunned. Therefore, he decided to use guerilla tactics, often attacking British targets at night. Gatunga and his forces utilized whatever they had at their disposal: not only guns but also machetes and even toxic gases.

The British viewed the guerilla style of fighting as primitive. In reality, though, it was smart. Not only did it allow the inferior Kenyan forces to inflict large casualties and achieve victories, but it was also not a style of fighting for which the British military was entirely prepared. While not unfamiliar from their centuries of colonization, many of the middle and high-ranking officers earned their stripes in

World War II, where more traditional battlefield fighting took place.

The inclusion of women and the often-brutal guerilla tactics only exacerbated the British opinion that the Mau Mau were backwards, even "savage." This led them to greatly misunderstand the causes of the uprising. In both their understanding of the rebellion and their response to it, they initially ignored the issues with land, taxes, labor, wages, and restrictions on freedoms that were the actual causes. Instead, to understand the reason why unrest broke out, they employed a psychiatrist named Dr. John Colin Carothers, who blamed the uprising on the Kenyans' primitive nature, as well as communist influences. This was a grave misunderstanding. The British launched a propaganda campaign on these premises among other Kenyans, but because they so deeply misunderstood the causes of the uprising, this campaign proved useless. While the Mau Mau tactics seemed radical—too radical to participate in—for most Kenyans, many were at least sympathetic to or supportive of their efforts in other ways.

Not only did the British misunderstand the causes of the rebellion, but they also delayed a serious reaction. The British government believed that because they were better supplied and trained, and generally superior to the Africans, the British army could easily put down this pesky uprising. It took them about a full year to take the uprising seriously. This delay allowed the Mau Mau to gain traction with less opposition.

Regardless, one of the first things the British did after the declaration of the state of emergency in October 1952 was to arrest many of the Mau Mau leaders that they knew of. They hoped to end the rebellion quickly by capturing and imprisoning them, hoping that the remaining Mau Mau would become disorganized and be forced to disband.

The day after the state of emergency was declared, 180 Mau Mau leaders were arrested in Nairobi. Dubbed Operation Jock Scott, this exercise proved to be a failure because information about it was leaked to the Mau Mau ahead of time. Knowing that they could not avoid some arrests, many of the important leaders fled to the forested regions of Kenya, and some (mostly mid-level) stayed behind and agreed to be arrested.

One of the prominent leaders who was arrested was Jomo Kenyatta. Kenyatta would go on to become Kenya's first prime minister after Kenya became independent. He was a member of the Kikuyu tribe and was an important figure before the rebellion, advocating for Kikuyu and Kenyan rights (particularly land rights).

Kenyatta and several other captured Mau Mau stood trial in 1953. The trial was a farce, and many violations of the Mau Mau fighters' rights to a fair trial were committed. Called the Kapenguria Six, all six of the most important leaders were convicted and spent much of the rest of the years of the rebellion in prison. This unfair trial served to further alienate average Kenyans from the British. However, it also gave Kenyatta the distance from the movement that would allow him to have such a successful political career afterward.

What happened in the immediate aftermath of Operation Jock Scott would help set the tone for the remainder of the conflict. The British established the Kenyan Home Guard, a militia unit of loyalist Kenyans who would become infamous for their use of torture practices against their fellow Kenyans. Then the British reinforced loyal Kenyan troops by summoning British battalions from other parts of Africa. They also sent a single battalion of British troops from Egypt, the Lancashire Fusiliers. This battalion was quite well-known and distinguished, especially for their service during the First and Second World Wars.

The Lancashire Fusiliers arrived on the day of Operation Jock Scott. The very next day, Senior Chief Nderi was murdered in broad daylight. He was allegedly killed by Mau Mau fighters when he tried to disband a group of 500 of them from organizing. They chopped his body into pieces, sending a clear message of retaliation. Over the next several weeks, the British returned brutality with more brutality, contributing to the tone of the rest of the conflict. In a rather random pattern, British troops and loyal Kenyan troops conducted a series of raids that often ended in the deaths of settlers. At the same time, Mau Mau operatives called for Kikuyu laborers on coffee farms to strike. Many Kenyan settlers may have previously been neutral before these attacks, but the brutal tactics used by the British alienated many more Kenyans from them. While they would not all join the fight against them, their loyalty was important in terms of support, tactical and otherwise. It made more Kenyans think favorably toward independence as well.

Operation Jock Scott and the sporadic arrival of more forces were attempts by the British to decapitate the movement early on. By 1954, though, the British recognized the Mau Mau Uprising as a serious threat, and their response finally became more aggressive. They ramped up military action and attempted to respond to some of the issues that caused the rebellion in the first place: land reform. They hoped that by doing so, they could squash the rebellion and ameliorate the majority of the Kenyan people, who were not involved in the war. Ultimately, both initiatives would prove insufficient.

Chapter Four

The British Respond: Operation Anvil

"Between 1952 and 1956, when the fighting was at its worst, the Kikuyu districts of Kenya became a police state in the very fullest sense of that term."

—David Anderson

The initial response on the part of the British was rather slow, even when colonial administrators and military officials in Kenya emphasized the need to take the Mau Mau Uprising more seriously. It was more than a year before Britain would back major initiatives. At that point, they decided to counter the uprising in three different ways.

First, they obviously had to deal with the Mau Mau fighters themselves. The mission to do so was named Operation Anvil and took aim at fighters headquartered in Nairobi. They primarily targeted the Kikuyu tribe, as they believed that most of the leaders and fighters were Kikuyu (even though there were a large number of members from other tribes). Then, they instituted a great deal of control over the Kikuyu in more rural parts of the country, outside of Nairobi, in a program called villagization. Finally, they attempted to address one of the major causes of the rebellion in the first place, land reform. They may have realized that without enacting real change and addressing this most egregious aspect of colonization, more rebellions would continue to spring up, even if the Mau Mau were defeated. This land reform initiative was called the Swynnerton Plan.

Operation Anvil began on April 24, 1954. It was technically over within two weeks, but for the captured Mau Mau suspects placed in camps, their ordeal was just beginning. British General George Erskine led Operation Anvil. He arrived in Kenya in June 1953 and began attacking Mau Mau almost immediately, though not in such an organized fashion as he would do with Operation Anvil.

The British knew that Operation Anvil needed to be swift. The Mau Mau benefited from the sympathy of the large Kikuyu population in Nairobi, and they knew that once the attack began, suspected Mau Mau would use the aid of sympathizers to escape. On January 15, 1954, the British captured Waruhiu Itote, an important Mau Mau leader. He had previously fled Nairobi with a group of followers and began launching raids against the colonial government from the region of Mount Kenya. It was during one of these raids against police in Mathira when he was shot in the neck and captured. In exchange for his life, he agreed to cooperate with the British, passing valuable information onto General Erskine that prompted and enabled Operation Anvil.

Originally, Erskine wanted to take more extreme measures. He wanted to remove all Kikuyu people from Nairobi, but the British government rejected that idea, believing it to be too extreme, with the potential to alienate more people and swell Mau Mau ranks. Meanwhile, rumors circulated throughout Nairobi about what the colonial government had planned in the days prior to Operation Anvil. They knew something was going to take place. Some Mau Mau leaders and fighters were able to flee the city before it commenced. In the early morning hours of April 24, four British battalions closed every road out of the city, as well as any footpaths, to prevent anyone from entering or exiting. Over the next several days, they swept through the city, arresting suspected Mau Mau and questioning more than 50,000 Kenyans (primarily Kikuyu). They were aided by Kikuyu informants who helped to identify the Mau Mau.

Operation Anvil had a tremendous impact on the city of Nairobi. A massive part of its labor force was removed, forcing a restructuring of the economy. It removed most of the unemployed Kenyans from the city as well, and this, too, affected the labor market. The British kept up their careful watch over Nairobi for several more months. Colonial administrators and security regularly questioned Kenyans who remained in the city, particularly Kikuyu members. Traffic and movement into and out of the city remained very restricted all the way through October.

For the KLFA, Operation Anvil was a serious blow. Many of the major leaders of the movement were scattered: either imprisoned or forced to subsist in the forest regions, miles from the kind of support they enjoyed in Nairobi. They eventually managed to re-group and resume their mission, but Operation Anvil was a drastic setback.

For the Mau Mau members who were captured, long years lay ahead of them; questioning continued, torture tactics were employed, and they were imprisoned in a series of camps (effectively concentration camps), described in a later chapter. The process of capturing and imprisoning so many Kenyans, particularly Kikuyu, also had a diasporic effect, as the colonial administration categorized the detainees into three broad categories. Detainees deemed loyal to the British (or at least not loyal to the Mau Mau) were mostly sent to live on reserves, while few were allowed to return to Nairobi. The British categorized them as "White." Below them were "Grey" detainees. These people expressed some views that could be considered loyal to the Mau Mau but were not active participants and deemed not likely to become active. Most were sent to the land reserves, some to camps, and a much smaller number were allowed to return to Nairobi.

As for the captured people who were loyal to the Mau Mau—or in the "Black" category—they faced a long road. The British set up a series of camps that these prisoners would have to move through. The first and highest-level work camp was the most harsh and brutal. As Kenyans showed improvements toward abandoning their revolutionary inclinations, they were theoretically supposed to be moved down through a series of work camps, each becoming less and less severe. In the end, the idea was for prisoners to move through all the work camps and be returned to land reserves, completely rehabilitated.

Operation Anvil was understandably terrifying for the people it targeted. The Swynnerton Plan, with which the British hoped to address the land issues, would prove to be somewhat more successful than previous land reform initiatives. It was put together by Roger Swynnerton, who worked for the Department of Agriculture. His idea was to redistribute Kenyan land, putting it back in the hands of Kenyan families. Each family farm would be large enough for both subsistence agriculture to support the families' food needs, with ample space to also produce a cash crop, such as coffee.

This plan had a dual purpose. First, it obviously served to quell unrest due to British land policies. If Britain was redistributing the land, and access to land was more fairly distributed between Kenyans and white settlers, what need would Kenyans have to rise up and fight, risking their lives and stability? For another, though, Britain aimed to keep Kenya in the global capitalist market. By making sure that most Kenyan farms still produced a cash crop, they better ensured their dependence on the market. Families would come to need the money from the cash crop to afford other necessities, like clothes and farming equipment. The best, safest, and easiest market for their cash crop was the west since supply chains and distribution networks were already in place. This dependence would make Kenyans—both then and in the future—less likely to align with communism.

This plan, however, was very much based on a western model of farming. Centuries earlier, most of Europe enclosed farms and enforced property boundaries. For native peoples in Kenya, this method was foreign. Land was held more communally, and the labor burden was shared among tribe members. While territoriality certainly existed, especially between tribes, land was not legally held in the same manner as had developed in Britain and across Europe.

This meant that the adoption of the Swynnerton Plan marked a sharp deviation from traditional patterns of landholding, farming, and relationships. The Kikuyu tribe in particular had always maintained this method of common land in order to protect the poor of their own kind: those poor still had access to land and a way to make a living. Never again would land be understood or treated in the same way. That way of life was virtually destroyed by the Swynnerton Plan.

In some ways, the Swynnerton Plan was a success. Land was consolidated and redistributed, and many Kenyans began making a living, being successfully converted to the western model of property and economics. What is more, the numbers bear this out: in the years following the implementation of the Swynnerton Plan, the number of cash crops produced in Kenya increased exponentially.

However, in other ways, it was also a failure. In essence, the Swynnerton Plan had two major downfalls: first, it did not do enough. White settlers still held most of the best land and held far more per capita than was redistributed to Kenyans. Also, the impact of the Swynnerton Plan socially was not welcomed by all. Suddenly, a large lower class emerged. These poor became destitute, unable to make a living or subsist. Interestingly, much the same thing happened in Europe after the enclosure of farmland. This new class of people divided tribes, virtually severing old tribal relationships. The social landscape of Kenya changed forever, and in the end, the Swynnerton Plan would not keep Kenya under British control.

The last major step taken by the British was a program of villagization. It was in essence a surveillance program meant to keep a very close watch on the Kikuyu in particular. Operation Anvil targeted the Kikuyu in Nairobi, while villagization took aim at rural Kikuyu. Through this program, the British hoped to prevent KLFA fighters from gaining a foothold anywhere outside Nairobi, now that they were dispersed. It also sought to root out Mau Mau sympathizers.

"Villagization" was the term that the British used, and ostensibly, it was put in place to protect loyal Kikuyu and rehabilitate those with KLFA sympathies. But what it actually was was a resettlement program to prevent supplies reaching Mau Mau fighters, and it aimed to punish sympathizers more than protect loyalists. Many of those resettled fell into the "Grey" category. The program was massive; in only a year and a half, more than one million Kikuyu were resettled. They were sent into "protected villages," but in actuality, the Kikuyu were anything but protected. These villages strictly restricted movement and were often surrounded by barbed wire. There was sometimes not enough space for all of the people housed inside of them, leading to problems caused by overcrowding, including starvation and disease. What was more, British resources were funneled much more into punishing the sympathizers than taking care of others.

Starvation was widespread in these villages, especially the ones ear-marked for Mau Mau sympathizers. Since nearly all Kikuyu were relocated, women and children also inhabited these villages and camps. Food shortages could not even be addressed by the Red Cross, and children were hit especially hard. More than 25,000 children perished from starvation, composing half of the total dead from starvation and malnutrition. Untold numbers faced lifelong health consequences due to malnutrition at an early age.

In the end, the villagization program was a massive failure for the British. While it was successful on paper—the Mau Mau were largely cut off from supplies, and probably a great many potential fighters were prevented from joining—in the long run, it greatly alienated Kikuyu people and Kenyans in general from the British. Most lost their land, livestock, and homes. Those who refused to be resettled watched the British destroy everything they had in an effort to force them into compliance. Many realized the drastic lengths that the British would go to in order to prevent Kenya from becoming independent and, instead of remaining loyal, realized how tenuous their livelihoods and lives were under British rule. In the coming years, this would swell support for independence and the Mau Mau.

Ultimately, all three initiatives of the British—Operation Anvil, the Swynnerton Plan, and villagization—would fail.

Chapter Five

Brutality and War Crimes

*"The main criticism we shall have to meet is that the plan,
which was approved by Government, contained
instructions which in effect authorized unlawful use of
violence against detainees."*

—Alan Lennox-Boyd, Colonial Secretary

No war in human history has ever escaped brutality. That said, the Mau Mau Uprising was especially vicious. Both sides committed atrocities. For the British, they used extreme measures to extract information from KLFA members, discourage support among civilians, and punish sympathizers. For the Mau Mau, they may have felt that the British deserved severe retaliation for the long history of mistreatment they had endured. They also responded ferociously against their own people who sided with the British.

It is important to remember that from the outset, the British viewed the Mau Mau Rebellion as a savage, backwards movement. They met its fighters accordingly. In addition, long-standing racism on the part of the colonial government and settlers existed toward all Kenyans, and they believed that they had to rule with an iron fist in order to maintain control.

The first thing that the British did that can be considered a war crime is the suspension of civil liberties. In general, all Kenyans suffered from restrictions on their rights. Probably the most egregious violations were committed against the Kikuyu people. Almost 500,000 were detained in camps, and over 1 million were forcibly relocated during the villagization program. This style of collective punishment alone violated the rights of many innocent people who had no revolutionary affiliations whatsoever.

The British retaliated against suspected Mau Mau sympathizers in other ways as well. As previously mentioned, many were rounded up and sent to labor camps. Sometimes, living and working conditions at these camps were very poor. What was more, when they were forcibly relocated to the camps, much of their property was stolen, including livestock, on which many were dependent for making a living. It was never returned, nor were they ever compensated.

The seizure of livestock was only the first in a series of hardships that Kenyans experienced during the years of the war. The camps were another arduous ordeal. As previously discussed, Kenyans were interrogated and sorted into one of three categories: White, Grey, or Black. The idea was that anyone at a higher level would be rehabilitated and moved. This system was dubbed "the Pipeline" by the British representative in charge, Thomas Askwith.

The system he developed was inherently flawed, however. Detainees were questioned and classified accordingly. However, the process of classification was anything but scientific. Detainees who divulged more information were generally considered more cooperative and often moved "down the Pipeline," while others who did not or could not give information were deemed uncooperative and sometimes sent to the higher-level camps. This system meant that intelligence collection on the part of the British was at times unreliable, as some Mau Mau would falsely confess or give other incorrect information just to be moved. It also caused great mistrust among the Mau Mau, as some of their previously loyal fighters and followers betrayed them to become spies, question suspected Mau Mau, or even participate in torture and beatings of their former comrades.

These betrayals and the suspicion that followed it also led to violence among the Mau Mau. When they discovered traitors in their midst, they reacted swiftly and violently: first strangling them to death and then defacing their bodies, often by cutting out their tongues. Many leaders also became paranoid about the people around them. When new prisoners in camps declined to declare an oath of loyalty to the Mau Mau, they were sometimes murdered. In turn, anyone suspected of administering oaths was executed by British authorities. The violence and killing only spread.

The methods of interrogation were also later declared war crimes. Very often, they were committed by members of the Kenya Home Guard. By the British allowing the Kenya Home Guard to do a great deal of their dirty work, the British would ostensibly avoid direct responsibility. However, the damage done to Kenya society lasted far beyond the period of colonization. Detainees were often beaten or tortured during questioning. Records contain evidence that fingers and other appendages were chopped off, some prisoners had their eardrums burned with cigarettes or their ears cut off. Women (and some men) were sexually assaulted, often using foreign objects. In worst-case scenarios, prisoners died during questioning— some deaths were accidental (beatings taken too far), while some prisoners were burned alive. More than one thousand suspected Mau Mau were hanged by the British for failure to participate. Some were shot on the spot in the camps when they failed to obey orders.

Initially, the Pipeline was fairly disorganized, but by 1956 at the latest, it operated like a well-oiled machine. The British had managed to streamline policies and develop more efficient, organized practices in order to maintain control over the residents and extract labor. At the lower levels on the Pipeline, labor was used in partial fulfillment of the Swynnerton Plan: detainees worked land producing subsistence crops as well as cash crops. At higher levels, forced labor was harsher and more brutal. Most of these higher-level camps provided labor to aid in the growth and construction of infrastructure in Kenya. They either manufactured necessary goods or sometimes provided labor for construction. At one infamous camp, the Embakasi Prison, detainees were forced to construct the Embakasi Airport. The project was wholly dependent on the forced labor; this meant that the people in charge of its construction felt the project must be completed before the state of emergency expired (when they would potentially lose their labor). Prisoners were forced to work long hours with few breaks and little food or water. It was one of the worst camps in the Pipeline.

As a whole, the conditions inside the camps were inhumane. Sanitation was a major issue, partially because the camps had been constructed in haste, partially because they quickly became overcrowded and overwhelmed, and partially because the British did not make the effort to keep them up. Diseases were rampant, and many detainees died from illnesses like typhoid. In addition, detainees were not properly fed, and many were malnourished. This exacerbated poor health and made the detainees more susceptible to disease. Conditions were sometimes so bad that camps closed; two camps, GilGil and Langata, were closed in 1955 because they were so filthy and so far gone that they were deemed beyond repair and unsuitable for habitation. In addition, at all levels of the camps and of the villagization program, violence and fear were still widespread. The Kenya Home Guard in particular grew notorious for their use of rape not only in interrogations but also randomly. Rape, beatings, and other acts of violence were perpetrated frequently by the Kenya Home Guard and their British overlords.

The process of being moved from one reserve to another was an ordeal onto itself. Depending where a prisoner was moving to and from, the trip could take several days, during which they were given little food and water.

The Mau Mau were certainly not innocent either. The fighters not detained in camps brought brutality down on the British, often attacking civilians. It led to a Catch-22; the British believed that the Mau Mau were savage by nature, and the viciousness of their attacks reinforced this view. The British then believed that they had to return the violence they encountered.

A few incidents committed by both the British and the Mau Mau have later been deemed massacres. The Lari Massacre resulted in the deaths of at least 74 Kikuyu people (including women and children) at the hands of their own on March 26, 1953. Mau Mau herded them into huts, under suspicion of British sympathies. They set the huts on fire and shot anyone who tried to flee.

Just a few months later, the Chuka Massacre took place on June 13, 1953, in the town of Chuka. British soldiers killed twenty unarmed men after they captured them as suspected Mau Mau sympathizers or fighters. It is still unclear why they were suspected, or what happened that prompted them to be massacred, and later, information showed that these people were actually loyalists of the Kikuyu Home Guard.

The Hola Massacre happened at one of the detention camps on March 3, 1959. This camp housed the most devoted KLFA fighters. Most of the men at this camp refused to divulge information, participate in the forced labor, or be "rehabilitated" in any way. British leadership at the camp decided they would force cooperation by selecting about ninety of the most obstinate Mau Mau and savagely beating them with clubs. Eleven men were killed, while the others suffered serious permanent injuries.

Because the Mau Mau Uprising was not a traditional war in the European sense, there was a tremendous amount of misinformation spread. In addition, not every British official participated in the torture or even supported it. The British attorney general for the colonial administration appealed to Governor Evelyn Baring about the use of torture on the part of their own troops. He compared their tactics to those of the USSR and Nazi Germany. However, he stopped short of asking for a cease of all physical violence, just that some tactics be stopped and less extreme measures be taken. He was quoted as saying, "If we must sin, we must sin quietly."

The British would not be able to keep the sins quiet forever. In 2012, the British government finally admitted to the commission of war crimes during the Mau Mau Uprising in Kenya.

Chapter Six

The End of the Rebellion

"I swear before God and before the people who are here that I have today become a soldier . . . and I will from now onwards fight the real fight for the land and freedom of our country till we get it or till my last drop of blood. Today I have set my first step as a warrior and I will never retreat."

—Excerpt from the Mau Mau Warrior Oath

Just as the exact date of the beginning of the Mau Mau Uprising is difficult to identify, the end date is also not definitive. Many place the date on October 21, 1956, when Dedan Kimathi, the most important leader of the rebellion at the time, was captured by the British. However, remnants of the Mau Mau Uprising continued after this point and even after Kenya achieved independence in 1963. After Kimathi's capture, Musa Mwariama, a member of the Meru tribe, led what was left of the rebellion. Most historians agree that it continued, officially at least, until 1960.

So, was the rebellion a success? Like so much of this war that is difficult to describe accurately, this question is also a difficult one to answer, partially because the exact objectives of the uprising are somewhat foggy. Certainly, the Mau Mau Uprising and the KLFA contributed to Kenyan independence in many ways. They laid bare and made it impossible to ignore the plight of Kenyan people in terms of land, labor, and rights. Some of these—particularly land—were addressed in response to the uprising.

Fighting the rebellion was extremely costly for the British, another factor that led to the end of the colonization of Kenya. It also demanded an immense amount of manpower. Hundreds of thousands of Kenyans, most of them Kikuyu, were forcibly relocated. The efforts toward organizing so many people into such a complicated system as the Pipeline, as well as maintaining control over the camps and settlements, was expensive and exhausting in itself.

The uprising was costly in other ways, too. The war was bloody; while it was far more deadly for Kenyans than for the British, in many ways it was a dirty war that tarnished Britain's reputation. Not only were Mau Mau fighters and sympathizers imprisoned in concentration camps, but civilians were also being massacred by both sides. These events impacted not only Britain's standing in Kenya but in other countries around the world. In other words, it became an effective propaganda tool for Britain's detractors.

This was further evidenced by the admission of war crimes by the British decades later. At a certain point, the British government and the colonial administration realized that holding onto Kenya, where further uprisings were probable, was no longer worth it. Even setting widespread torture and violence aside, the Mau Mau Uprising was very bloody. The British used capital punishment liberally, executing almost 1,100 Kenyans. In total, more than 20,000 Mau Mau were killed in the conflict.

These numbers say nothing of the actual probable number of casualties though. This number is widely disputed among ethnographers and historians. The highest estimates put the Kikuyu dead in the hundred thousands—somewhere between 130,000 and 300,000. While it is hard to establish a firm number of Kikuyu and Kenyan dead, that point alone reinforces the fact that the war was experienced and understood differently by different peoples.

Independence for Kenya became all the more timely during the period of decolonization for Africa and colonies around the world. Part of the impetus for decolonization was fear of communism. It was understood that if Britain continued to force control in Kenya, Kenyans may turn to communist powers for aid in their fight. The British already believed that communists were influencing the KLFA. It was better to let them go, while maintaining some of their economic dependency on the west, than to let them fall to communism.

The impact of the Mau Mau Uprising on independence is further evidenced by the fact that Jomo Kenyatta, an early KLFA leader imprisoned by the British in Operation Jock Scott, became Kenya's first prime minister. Recognized as a revolutionary leader, Kenyatta seemed a natural continuation for Kenya. In addition, since he was imprisoned early in the conflict, he was not directly involved in some of the more brutal fighting, keeping his reputation clean.

Fighting in Kenya did not end with independence, and it was not a smooth transition to nationhood. Unfortunately, this is one of the common legacies of colonization globally.

The Mau Mau Uprising had damaged inter- and intra-tribal relations and further divided the people of the region. This was especially true for the Kikuyu, who had hunted and slaughtered each other during the conflict. In addition, it was unclear what the status of landholding would be after the British evacuated, especially concerning whether or not white settlers would keep their land.

Upon independence, a legislative body was established with 66 seats. Half of them were designated for black Kenyans and half for other groups, which was in itself an issue since ethnicity in Kenya was anything but black and white. In fact, a rebellion in the northern regions of the country sprang up almost immediately. The new Kenyan government had to contend with ethnic Somali. Fighting continued for more than six years, until Kenyatta essentially became an autocrat, establishing a one-party system. Corruption ran rampant and election fraud plagued the new nation.

In the end, the Mau Mau Uprising contributed to ousting the British and awarding Kenya independence. However, in the ensuing decades, historians and Kenyans alike have had to grapple with the question of the cost. The Mau Mau Uprising has had an enduring legacy for the British but especially within Kenya itself.

Chapter Seven

Legacy

"We are determined to have independence in peace, and we shall not allow hooligans to rule Kenya. We must have no hatred towards one another. Mau Mau was a disease which had been eradicated, and must never be remembered again."

—Jomo Kenyatta

The significance of the Mau Mau Uprising in Kenya's history, as well as the history of colonialism, the British Empire, African history, and Kenyan culture, is very much unclear and widely debated by Kenyans and historians alike.

When the uprising began, the British worked hard to paint it as a small movement by a radical sect, which was savage and backwards. They launched a propaganda campaign against the Mau Mau to prevent other Kenyans from joining them. They also went to great lengths to contain the movement, imprisoning and relocating the vast majority of Kikuyu people, as well as members from other tribes.

While historians look back on this aspect of the uprising and recognize it as rooted in colonial racism, its impact on the Kenyan people is more nuanced. For decades (and in some cases, centuries), colonized peoples were told that they were inferior, stunted, and savage. They were forced to forsake long-held traditions and practices and were taught that westernization was inherently good while their culture was inherently bad.

The fact that the British pushed this message associated with the Mau Mau Rebellion and the KLFA makes it difficult to reconcile in the larger story of Kenyan history. In addition, the fact that it was led and fought by a relative minority of Kenyans means that it has been difficult for the majority of Kenyans to adopt personally, especially since it is still a relatively recent event. Finally, it did not result immediately in independence, so it cannot hold the place in Kenyan culture that other wars of revolution do for other nations.

The negative views of the Mau Mau Uprising have been challenged, however. Most notably, in the decades after the uprising, Mau Mau members wrote several memoirs and books about the rebellion. They described events that the British had hidden or downplayed, and they expressed the Mau Mau vision more coherently. It was clear from most of these works that the Mau Mau did, in fact, have the independence of Kenya on their agenda. Most of them also argued the importance of the Mau Mau movement to the history of Kenya as a whole and the establishment of its national identity.

Clearly, the former Mau Mau fighters had a biased point of view. But even if unrepresentative of the greater population of Kenya, the Mau Mau Uprising certainly played a role in Kenyan independence. It pushed issues like land reform to the forefront and cost the British more than just money. It also raised awareness and gave voice within and without Kenya about the ways that native peoples had suffered and experienced loss and discrimination under British rule. In the twenty-first century, Mau Mau veterans' organizations exist, and former fighters seem to be proud of their work toward Kenyan independence.

Conclusion

The Mau Mau Uprising, which began in 1952 and ended around 1960, has had an impact long beyond its eight-year history. It is also an abundantly difficult event to describe since so much of its meaning is disputed among Kenyans and historians alike.

What is clear is that the Mau Mau Uprising is an important event for a variety of reasons. Certainly, Kenyan national history and especially Kenya's independence cannot be properly understood without it. While the majority of Kenyans were not participants in the conflict, and their level of support is still largely unclear, leaving it out of any telling of those two stories would be an egregious error.

In many ways, the division within and without Kenya about the Mau Mau Uprising reflects one of the biggest challenges that colonization—and, eventually, decolonization—caused around the world. What is now called Kenya was formed largely by European territoriality instead of organically as a nation.

The KLFA fighters in the Mau Mau Uprising may have intended to reconcile that issue by forming a movement Kenyans could support together. Many of them declare as much in their memoirs, but others disagree. Regardless of this issue, what is clear and undisputed is that the Mau Mau Uprising is abundantly important in the story of Kenya as a nation.

Bibliography

Anderson, David (2005). Histories of the Hanged.

Blakeley, Ruth (2009). State Terrorism and Neoliberalism: The North in the South.

Furedi, Frank (1989). The Mau Mau War in Perspective.

Kanogo, Tabitha (1992). Dedan Kimathi: A Biography.

Kariuki, Josiah Mwangi (1975). "Mau Mau" Detainee: The Account by a Kenya African of his Experiences in Detention Camps 1953–1960.

Maloba, Wunyabari O. (1998). Mau Mau and Kenya: An Analysis of a Peasant Revolt.

Mumford, Andrew (2012). The Counter-Insurgency Myth: The British Experience of Irregular Warfare.

Page, Malcolm (2011). King's African Rifles: A History.

Printed in Great Britain
by Amazon

32827129R00030